Amgueddfa Genedlaethol Cymru
National Museum of Wales
Cardiff 1993

Welsh Country Workers Housing 1775-1875

by Jeremy Lowe

Acknowledgements

Illustrations: 16, 29, Clwyd Record Office; 8, Peter Hayes (and Clwyd Record Office); 4, Gwynedd Archives; 35, Mrs James; 28, Simon Unwin; 19, Welsh Folk Museum; all others by the author. Drawings by the author from his own surveys, except as follows: 6, based on data from Maredudd ab Iestyn and Margaret Griffith; 8, Peter Hayes; 12, Royal Commission on Ancient and Historical Monuments in Wales; 23, Corporation of Trinity House; 29, Clwyd Record Office; 37, Welsh School of Architecture.

I wish to thank David G. Jones, for his help with houses in Dyfed, Dr. Eurwyn Wiliam and Gerallt Nash (Welsh Folk Museum), Tony Parkinson (RCAHM) and the staffs of the National Library of Wales and of the Clwyd, Glamorgan, Gwent and Gwynedd Archives for their generous help. I am indebted to all the owners and occupiers of the houses illustrated and to Margaret Griffith, Peter Hayes, David Parr, Captain Parry and the Corporation of Trinity House for their specific contributions to this booklet.

Jeremy Lowe, Welsh School of Architecture
March 1985

Access: There is access to only three of these houses: Penparcau Tollhouse at the Welsh Folk Museum, St Fagans *(page 19)*, the Pilots Cottages, Llanddwyn Island *(pages 24/25)*, and the Junction House, Pont-y-moel *(page 26)*. The others are all private dwellings to which there is no access; please do not disturb the occupants.

Introduction

This booklet is a companion to **Welsh Industrial Workers Housing 1775-1875**, first published by the National Museum of Wales in 1977. It illustrates the homes of workers who lived in the countryside of Wales during the first century of the industrial revolution. Most were farm labourers, but there were also country craftsmen, the smiths and wrights who made farm tools, equipment and machinery, the spinners and weavers who produced the homespun cloth of the countryside, the tanners and workers in leather, and the makers of articles in wood, basketwork and pottery. All these were long established crafts, given new impetus by changes in agriculture and the growth in the use of iron during the 18th century. There were also new occupations, most of which in the country were connected with transport. Toll-roads, canals and eventually the railways, created a need for specialised housing, taking workers to many isolated places.

Nineteenth century travellers described for us the country living conditions of their day. Their impressions varied widely. Some idealised the cottage, portraying it as the most attractive of dwellings, with its dainty windows, its broad-spreading roof and big chimney, its low-ceilinged rooms cosy in winter, its garden bright with flowers in summer. Thus in 1838 William Howitt wrote in *The Rural Life of England* "these rustic abodes must inspire us with ideas of a peace and purity of life in soothing contrast to the luxury and immorality of cities". In 1903 A. G. Bradley described the earth-walled and thatched cottages of central Dyfed, in *Highways and Byways in South Wales,* as "the quaintest and most picturesque in the world . . . the roof is a thing of joy and a work of art that throws . . . the best of their kind known to me in England hopelessly in the shade". He added, regretfully, "fifty years hence there will probably be none left", and so it is.

Other writers looked through the apparent softness of the country cottage and saw the hard reality of the life within. For all their outward charm many cottages were ill-built and ill-kept, lacking comfort and convenience, the home in too many cases of ignorance, destitution, dirt and distress. In *Cruel Habitations* Enid Gauldie quotes what Richard Cobden told Parliament in 1844. Welsh farm labourers, he said, lived in "mud huts, with only one room for sleeping, cooking and living, the different ages and sexes herding together. Their cottages have no windows, only a hole through the mud wall into which a bundle of rags or a turf is thrust at night. The thinly thatched roofs are seldom drop-dry and the mud-floors become damp and dirty almost as the road; to complete the wretched picture, huddled in a corner are the rags and straw of which their beds are composed". Bad conditions were still regarded officially as a natural feature of country dwellings only sixty years ago. A report on the district south-west of

Snowdon in the 1920s remarks flatly that in "houses of the small cottage type such as are occupied by farm labourers in agricultural districts, defects in sanitary arrangements, water supply and in facilities for the disposal of refuse are not of such vital importance". So in reality country cottage life varied from the rural idyll to the rural slum.

We do not know for certain when solid, durable houses were first built for ordinary farm labourers in Wales. Up to the eighteenth century it was the Welsh custom that farm workers were engaged by the year. They were given meals in the farmhouse kitchen and if unmarried slept in the lofts over the house and its outbuildings. Such workers had few clothes and fewer possessions and needed only the most basic accommodation. Only those who took the bold step of marrying would have lived, with their families, in homes of their own. Home was in any case a shifting concept around many upland parts of Wales. The practice of "transhumance", the movement in summer of flocks and herds to hill pastures, continued well into the eighteenth century, and several of the *hafotai*, the summer farmhouses, were still in regular use in 1775.

In the mid-eighteenth century the idea that farm workers should all live out began to seep slowly through Wales. From their English neighbours, prosperous border farmers took up the idea that it was not seemly to eat with their farm labourers, nor to have them sleeping under the same roof as their own families. More important, they found that outworkers could be employed by the week, and laid off without pay when the weather was bad or work was slack. They still provided meals, but in a separate room. The labourers took lodgings or built themselves homes where they could. Neither owners nor tenants — ninety per cent of farmers were tenants — were willing to build houses for any but the most essential workers.

Few labourers had the skill to build themselves proper houses, or the resources to employ a professional builder, even if they could acquire a suitable site. So there grew up a widespread scatter of poorly built 'squatter' cabins, on sites made by 'encroachment' on the grass verges of public roads or on common land. Welsh custom allowed a man to live on common land if he could erect a *tŷ unnos*, a house built in one night. Such houses were bound to be poorly built and the lawful proprietors of the commons preferred that they should be so. They tolerated the squatters because it suited them to do so. In the nineteenth century, most of the commons were enclosed and many of the squatters lost such 'rights' as Welsh custom had given them. They became once more rent paying tenants of the big landowners or they were evicted so that their homes could be demolished and the land repossessed for farming.

Many squatter sites can still be identified, mostly at the roadside, but the houses now on them were erected by local builders, with the permission of the land owner. Who paid for labourers houses is hard to discover. Those which were sited on farmland would have been financed by the tenant farmers, who usually had lifetime leases. A roadside cottage north of Aber-cuch (Dyfed) has an inscription stone reading "Glantivy was built by the tenant 1854 D + O". In Gwent and eastern Clwyd the first permanent cottages may have been built as early as 1700. Certainly by 1775 a few labourers houses, built in stone or timber framing, could be seen in eastern areas. In the rest of Wales, rough rubble stonework and materials like *clom* — earth compacted with straw — were used until well into the nineteenth century for the building of cottages to replace the squatters huts. By 1875 the railways were reaching even remote corners of Wales. They permitted local builders to use industrial materials, like bricks and machine-sawn softwood, for housing.

Our appreciation of the historic interest of workers houses is fairly new. Few of the cottages illustrated have been protected by an official 'listing', nor have they been recorded in any detail. The humble people who lived in them left few marks upon the historical record of their day, but their houses remain as vital evidence of their lives. Much of this evidence is disappearing under the pressure of house improvement. The prophecy that the thatched roofs of Dyfed would vanish has come true. Soon *clom* walling will be gone too. Re-roofed, re-windowed, re-doored, re-plastered, re-painted, the cottages of Wales are losing character and historic value. It is almost too late to record all their physical and pictorial variety.

The booklet is in three main sections. First come some of the basic housing types of the late eighteenth and early nineteenth centuries. Next are pictures and plans of houses built for craftsmen and other workers in specialised occupations. The third section shows houses of the industrial age, ranging from simple dwellings to elaborate houses built on large country estates.

Drawing Scale: To help comparison of the sizes, areas and volumes of the houses shown in this booklet, their plans and sections are all reproduced to the same scale of 1 : 250 (10 mm represents 2.5 m). The vertical scale line beside each cross-section is divided into metres and tenths of a metre.

Some Basic House Types

The simplest form of cottage in Wales was the single-room dwelling, with one undivided space, earth-floored, rough-walled, open to the sloping underside of the roof. Construction was also simple. William Bingley, who toured North Wales in 1798 and 1801, described the homes of the poorest people as "huts built of stones whose interstices are closed with peat or mud". At Rhaeadr, writes Iorwerth Peate in *The Welsh House,* the walls of one-room houses were made of clods of turf, and on the Merioneth and Montgomeryshire border of rough branches woven into some sort of framework and plastered over with mud. The roofs were formed of the same kind of timbers, thatched with heather, bracken or straw, or even covered with turf. Such houses were in the tradition of the *tai unnos,* the squatters cabins of the pre-enclosure period. Few permanent houses were built in one-room form.

Inside each single-roomed house were gathered the possessions of a whole family, their primitive furniture and beds, their few clothes and blankets, their store of food (little though that might be), their cooking and eating utensils, and such tools and equipment as they used in their daily work. Tent campers will have an idea of such a life. Some houses had no windows. In others the windows were very small, mere holes closed with tiny fixed panes of glass or just protected against the worst of the weather by a bundle of heather. Stone houses had fireplaces and chimneys. Bingley said that the chimneys usually admitted more light than the windows. Mud and timber houses might have only a central hearth within the room, from which smoke escaped by a vent hole somewhere in the roof or through the wickerwork of the walls "after mellowing every article of furniture as well as the complexions of the inmates" wrote Sir Daniel Lleufer Thomas in 1893. Decrepit dwellings of this kind fell into disuse during the later nineteenth century. Most were deliberately destroyed by the landowners, after the eviction of the cottagers. Any that were abandoned would soon have disappeared, such useful materials as they contained being carried off elsewhere. A few were sketched by travellers, or included in picturesque landscape paintings, but not with enough detail to give us a clear impression of their form.

We know from visitors to Wales that some simple cottages were kept neat and tidy. George Borrow, walking across Anglesey in 1854, was shown into a cottage at Penmynydd by a husband and wife. "We sat down", he wrote, "on stools by a clean white table in a little apartment with a clay floor". Earlier, in the eighteenth century, William Hutton wrote of a cottage interior with two beds, tables and cupboards, and shelves of crockery, all kept clean and orderly, "polished by the hand of industry". Of course not every householder managed to reach such a standard. In 1798 William Bingley ate a lunch of bread and butter in a cottage at Llanberis from a table "covered with a dirty napkin" in the company, not only of the cottager and his family, but also "a large overgrown old sow devouring her dinner, with considerable dissatisfaction on account of the short allowance, from a pail placed for her by the daughter in one corner of the room". Bingley took pains to emphasise that the cottager was not a native of North Wales.

Illustrating what one-roomed interiors looked like is this picture of **Jane Williams's Cottage,** on **Bardsey Island** (Gwynedd), photographed about 1910. Hers was a two-roomed house built in the later nineteenth century. But it offers a fair impression of the single living space, with its equipment for daily life. The furniture is rough and heavy, made by a carpenter and passed down from one owner to another. No chair can be seen, only a settle whose back is draped with some clothing or bed-covering. There is also a three-legged stool, supporting a box. The solid dresser is crowded with cups and plates; bottles and jars are ranged along its top shelf and under the two drawers. In the corner are several large tubs and bowls, perhaps to store durable provisions, and a broom. A heavy cooking pot is balanced over the brick-sided fire grate. On the mantelpiece above the fire, as much as possible out of the reach of mice, are food jars and boxes as well as a washing bowl. On the wall hangs Jane Williams's spinning wheel and, in the upper corner, a fishing net with floats. In a actual one-roomed cottage there would have been at least one bed, but we see none, because this house had a separate bedroom. We shall be following, in the next few pages, the way in which the cottage plan developed by the separation of spaces for different uses and activities.

An early development of the one-room house was the formation of a space for sleeping. There were two simple ways in which this could be done. One was by horizontal addition. The sleeping room was placed next to the main living area, on the same level. This produced a rectangular plan divided into two main 'units', one for living, one for sleeping. The other method was to put the sleeping area over the living space, making a building roughly square on plan.

Bwlchygarreg, Rhiw (Gwynedd), in the Lleyn Peninsula, is a cottage of the two-unit type. Such rectangular houses were being built in Wales early in the eighteenth century. They were never common in the eastern borderlands though a few survived until quite recent times in Gwent and Clwyd. Today they are found almost exclusively in the west, in Gwynedd and Dyfed. Bwlchygarreg, which is typical of such houses, was built before 1816. Though farm buildings have since been added *(on the right)* it was once a true worker's house. The 1841 census, the first to record individual occupations and ages, shows that Humphrey Rowland, an agricultural labourer aged 49, lived there with his wife Margred, also 49, their two young children and a woman aged at least 80, perhaps Margred's mother. The house is a classic example of North-west Welsh building. It has one door, roughly (but not exactly) in the centre of one long side. Flanking the door are two little windows, again roughly but not quite symmetrical in size and position. The rubble stone walls have massive boulders at their base. The roof is covered in small slates, the cheapest output of the great Snowdonian quarries, and the ridge line ends in a solid square stone chimney.

In 1937 Llewelyn Wyn Griffith, in *The Wooden Spoon,* described another cottage of this type, then standing only a few hundred metres from Bwlchygarreg. "As you enter through the door, the kitchen is on your right: a small room with no ceiling between the floor and the roof. On the right of the door as you enter is a wooden partition, three feet wide and six feet high, to keep out the cold. On the left as you go in there is a wooden partition running up to the roof with two doors in it, one vertically above the other. Through the lower door you enter the bedroom: this has a wooden ceiling which serves as a floor to the attic above. To get to the attic bedroom you pull down a ladder which normally lies on the attic floor. These are the three rooms of the cottage". Bwlchygarreg, following this layout, thus has two rooms in the sleeping 'unit', one above the other.

There was a need for one more space, a food store or *bwtri*. In Bwlchygarreg this space was partitioned off beside the downstairs bedroom but in other two-unit houses it is placed in the corner next to the fireplace. The upper sleeping space, called an attic by Llewelyn Wyn Griffith, has become known now as the *croglofft*. Houses of this kind are often called 'croglofft cottages'.

Before the 1861 census, Bwlchygarreg became the home of Isaac Roberts, his wife and their seven children. He was a farmer, and later the joint owner of a small manganese mine. His descendants lived in the house until just before the Second World War.

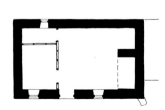

Ground Floor

Cross Section

The two-unit cottage was very much less common in Eastern Wales and usually took a rather different form. The entrance was at one end, into a lobby beside the fireplace. Sir Cyril Fox and Lord Raglan recorded two houses of this type in Gwent which were built, they thought, about 1700. Both houses had the doorway to the lobby in the gable wall, locally called the 'pine' or 'pyne' end. In Clwyd and Powys the doorway was usually in the front wall.

The Old Toffee Shop, Hawarden (Clwyd) illustrates the lobby-entry plan with the door in the front wall. This cottage had the simplest form of two-unit plan. The roof was thatched and its underside was once entirely open to the rooms below. There was a shallow step up into the bedroom but no sign of any *croglofft*. The Old Toffee Shop was certainly built before 1815, quite probably around the middle of the eighteenth century. It was one of a group of old cottages in the Hawarden district, possibly related to the beginnings of industry in that area. The two brick chimneys and the bedroom fireplace were later additions. The cottage was demolished some years ago.

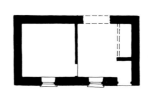

Ground Floor

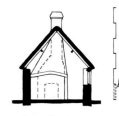

Cross Section

Porth-eiddy Cottage, near **Llanrhian** (Dyfed) stands a little way inland from the Pembrokeshire coast. It was near the main farmhouse at Porth-eiddy, but faced away from it. This gave the farmhouse some privacy while exposing the cottage to westerly gales. Like many other houses on the West coast, the cottage roof was completely cemented over and lime-washed as a protection against driving rain. Porth-eiddy cottage was built before 1845. As first built it had a loft room lit by the little window in the gable. The 'dormer' windows were added about 1920 when the inside was rebuilt with a full first floor. The white paint is recent. Red, orange and pink, ''colours of life, blood and sun'' writes Peter Smith, were traditional. They were made by mixing *lliw coch,* the red raddle used for marking sheep, or ochre into the limewash. A patch of orange can be seen on this house, where the white is peeling away.

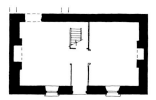

Ground Floor

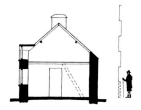

Cross Section

The two-unit cottage gradually developed in the nineteenth century into a house type with a complete first floor. This feature can be identified by the narrow winding staircase which is usually placed beside the living room fireplace. In larger cottages the first floor space would be split by a boarded partition into two rooms. That arrangement gave the girls in the family a separate sleeping space, though they still had to go through the boys' space to reach their own bedroom.

Ty'n-rhyd, in **Llanrhystud Anhwniog** parish (Dyfed) was built after 1841. It is one of a group of lobby-entry cottages to be found in South Cardiganshire. It is interesting also in having its main windows on the opposite side of the house to the entrance. They face south-west. This direction was traditionally considered unhealthy because southerly winds were thought to be plague-infected. There were practical objections too. The architect John Wood in his *Series of Plans for Cottages* of 1781 advised against west-facing rooms. Later John Claudius Loudon, the encyclopaedist, suggested the choice of an easterly orientation. Both authors knew that outdoor farm workers sought the comfort of a cool shaded room after spending a long hot summer day toiling in the fields.

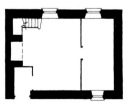

Ground Floor

Cross Section

There was a house at **Cwmsidan, Maenordeifi** (Dyfed) before 1814, but the cottage we see there today was built much later in the 19th century after bricks had become commonly available in West Wales. The 'quoins' or corners of the building and all the window and door surrounds are made of brickwork, thus avoiding skilled stone cutting. Cwmsidan followed the traditional plan of the region, but it had also a full first floor, divided into two bedrooms, and a 'lean-to' *bwtri* or larder projecting at the back. The wide main fireplace was covered by the traditional hood made of wicker-work. This was plastered with mud inside and outside and sloped upwards into the first floor space. In 1841 the census recorded that David Isaac and his wife Mary lived at the original Cwmsidan. He was an agricultural labourer, aged 26, and she was about 20. They had two sons: James, aged 2, and William, 3 months.

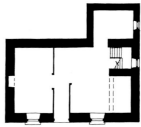

Ground Floor

Cross Section

Alternative to the two-unit plan is the one-down, one-up cottage, much more common in Eastern Wales than in the West. The basic plan shape is more-or-less square. So the house seems to be cut out of a cube with the two upper edges sliced off to make the roof slopes. This type, like the two-unit cottage, dates back at least to the eighteenth century. A 'cube' house was built in the parish of Hawarden (Clwyd) before 1740. The house shown on this page, **Diana Cottage, Merthyr Mawr** (Glamorgan) may be older still. It has been much altered inside but keeps its thatched roof. In the other picture *(right)* we see a later, much smaller, example of the 'cube' cottage. **The Nutshell, Crossgates** (Powys), in the parish of Llanbadarn Fawr, was built after 1840 but before 1887, on a site resulting from the diversion of a farm road. This tiny house, the smallest in this booklet, has a floor area of only 21.8 square metres. It has two walls of brickwork and two of timber framing covered with roughly sawn horizontal boards. Various single storey additions allowed the house to remain in use until the 1980s. The dormer window lighting the first floor bedroom is an original feature of the design.

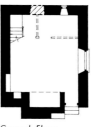

Ground Floor

Ground Floor   Cross Section

The Cottage, Pool Road, Berriew (Powys) illustrates the 'cube' cottage in timber construction. It has the lobby entry commonly found in the East of Wales and dates from the early 19th century. One wall, with the fireplace and chimney, is built of bricks and the other three are framed in timber with either plastered infill panels or boarded cladding. The front wall was skilfully constructed as a series of square panels, now rather disrupted by changes to the window and door openings. This cottage was probably built about the same time as the nearby Limekiln Houses at Belan Locks, near Welshpool *(page 33).*

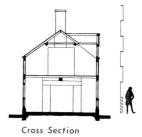

Ground Floor   Cross Section

Glantwymyn, Bontdolgadfan (Powys) in the parish of Llanbryn-mair is built of stone. It stands on unenclosed land at the junction of the Wern brook *(see page 28)* with the Twymyn river. It is one of the most westerly examples of the cube cottage, with a lobby entry, and is a larger and more complex version of the basic two-room form. Behind the small square living room, with its wide fireplace, is a narrow service room. This house was probably built about 1820 or 1830, when the little village was a busy centre of wool spinning and weaving. By the mid-century employment in weaving in the countryside had greatly declined. Most workers in Bontdolgadfan were then occupied in farming or as lead miners at Dylife.

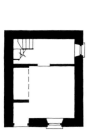

Ground Floor

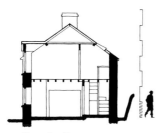

Cross Section

Frances Gray.

Section 2 New Jobs in the Countryside

In the two centuries before 1775 industrial development had had only a small effect on most of the Welsh countryside. In a few scattered places charcoal burning iron furnaces had been started up, in the west and north some small metal mines had opened and around Swansea and Holywell copper smelting was established. Otherwise Wales was an agricultural land. The production of woollen cloth was its only widespread exporting industry, for the lack of good transport held back other industrial development. Many roads were unfit for wheeled vehicles. Fat cattle and sheep could be walked to their markets along green 'drovers' roads and trackways. Cloth could be carried to Shrewsbury by pack horse. But heavy and bulky materials such as iron ore, coal, or limestone could only be carried economically by water. For a long time heavy industry had to be sited near the coast or on stretches of river accessible from the sea. This situation began to change in the years 1770 to 1800 when the building of canals opened up new industrial areas in South Wales. But most of the country was too undulating for canal construction. It was the turnpike road system which first brought better transport to most country areas.

The turnpikes were gates at which tolls were collected by public trusts for building and maintaining main roads. The system grew gradually across Wales from the 1760s onwards, its most spectacular feature being the re-building of the Holyhead road (the modern A5) by Thomas Telford between 1815 and 1826. The gates and tolls remained until the 1870s. Many of the gatekeepers houses can still be seen but mostly they are of nineteenth century construction. At first the revenues of the trusts were small. They limited their work to improvement of the road surface, previously often a mass of ruts and potholes, and to making diversions round the steepest hills. The shelters provided for their toll-bar keepers were often simple, scarcely more than huts or cabins.

The **Llwynegrin Gate** (left) was north-east of **Mold** (Clwyd) on a road diversion built after 1839. The little cabin was a one-room shelter for the gatekeeper who had to turn out at all hours to collect tolls from passing travellers. Walkers used the turnstile to pass without payment. On the gable wall of the toll-house a large board listed the charges to be paid. **Llandegai Gate**, near **Llandegai** (Gwynedd) is a more elaborate building which was designed by Thomas Telford, one of the series of toll-houses along his Holyhead road. A brick house to this design is preserved at the Ironbridge Gorge Museum (Shropshire). The Llandegai house was built in stone about 1825. It has shelters for the gatekeeper on both sides of the carriageway. The arched recess held the board listing the toll charges.

The specially designed toll-house is often easily recognised, but many other toll-houses were indistinguishable from ordinary roadside cottages. They were built in many sizes and many shapes. One of the last to be built in Wales stands beside the A470 near Pontdolgoch, north-west of Caersws (Powys). When the Llanidloes and Newtown Railway was opened in 1859 a new spur road was constructed linking the turnpike from Machynlleth through Llanwnog to Newtown to the railway line south-east of Caersws. The line of the Llanwnog road has since been changed but the house shows where the two roads joined.

Old Toll-gate Cottage, Llanllwchaiarn (Powys) was built in the early 1820s after the opening of the final section of the Montgomeryshire Canal to its Newtown terminus. It introduces us to another common type of cottage which combined features of both basic types shown in Section One. It has no special features to indicate its original purpose. Over a squarish ground floor, divided into two small rooms, cottages of this kind have one or two first floor bedrooms, lit by windows in the gable walls. They have a practical four-square solidity, expressing the ideas of the coming industrial age. The house has been much altered since this picture was taken. The decision to set up the two **Penparcau Gates,** near **Aberystwyth** (Dyfed) was taken in November 1771. The toll-house which stood between them was finished on March 23rd 1772. It is now preserved at the Welsh Folk Museum, St Fagans, Cardiff. The single-room interior *(right)* has been furnished quite richly. Few toll-bar keepers would have owned so many attractive possessions at the time when the toll-house was built. Of special interest are the massive box-bed on the left, and the rush-light holder hanging from the ceiling beam.

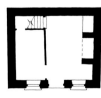
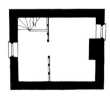
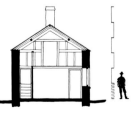

Ground Floor   First Floor   Cross Section

Many of the toll-houses that survive today can be found on sections of main road that have since been by-passed to remove a series of corners or ease out a steep gradient. This process of improvement has gone on intermittently ever since the turnpike trusts were first set up. Their purpose was to take main roads out of purely local, parish, control into the care of an authority more concerned with the long distance traveller. In practice it was the local users who resented the tolls they now had to pay on farm produce, lime and manure. Even more they disliked the way the number of gates increased as the turnpike system developed. In 1843, after a period of serious economic slump, rioting against the tolls broke out in South Wales. Farmers and smallholders, in gangs led by a mysterious 'Rebecca', wearing masks and other disguises, attacked toll-houses at night. The worst riots occurred in Carmarthenshire but in Glamorgan too gates were destroyed and keepers brutally assaulted. As a result the whole turnpike system was centralised and then gradually abolished over the next 30 years.

The Old Toll-house, Llanfaches (Gwent) stands on a by-passed section of the main Chepstow-Newport road. Its Regency Gothick style is typical of the 1820s. This was the last gate in the Chepstow District of the Monmouthshire turnpikes. Westwards of this point the main road was maintained by the Newport District, which used a different Tudor-style toll-house design, to be seen today at Caerleon Bridge. The Monmouthshire Trust was set up in 1758, but this toll-house was probably part of a general improvement of the Chepstow to Newport road authorised by Act of Parliament in 1811. In 1841 the only person living in the toll-house was the 60 year old gatekeeper, John Gabb. Two years later he would have felt very vulnerable to attack in his lonely situation.

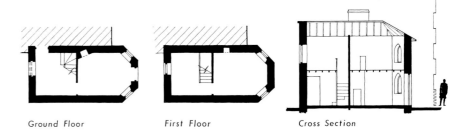

Ground Floor   First Floor   Cross Section

Tolls to be taken at LLANFAIR GATE.

	s. d
For every Horse, Mule, or other Cattle drawing any Coach or other Carriage with springs the sum of	4
For every Horse, Mule or other Beast or Cattle drawing any Waggon, Cart, or other such Carriage not employed solely in carrying or going empty to fetch Lime for manure the sum of	3
For every Horse, Mule, or other Beast or Cattle, drawing any Waggon, Cart, or other such Carriage, employed solely in carrying or going empty to fetch Lime for manure the sum of	1½
For every Horse, Mule or Ass, laden or unladen, and not drawing, the sum of	1
For every Drove of Oxen, Cows, or other neat Cattle per score, the sum of	10
For every Drove of Calves, Sheep, Lambs, or Pigs per score, the sum of	3

For every Horse, Mule, or other Beast drawing any Waggon, or Cart, the Wheels being less than 3 inches in breadth, or having Wheels with Tires fastened with Nails projecting and not countersunk to pay double Toll.

A Ticket taken here clears Carnedd Du Bar.

The Toll-house, Llanfair-pwllgwyngyll (Anglesey), also stands on Thomas Telford's Holyhead road. It may have been designed by him. It was built about 1823, ready for the opening of the Menai Bridge in 1826. Several similar houses survive along the road to Holyhead. This one is particularly well preserved and even carries its old toll-board. In 1841 William and Margaret Jones lived there with their five children, aged between 10 years and 10 months. He was 32 years old; his occupation is given as 'bootbinder', that is a cobbler. Such a trade could be combined with the duties of a gatekeeper to supplement the meagre wage which was probably not enough for the support of a family of seven people.

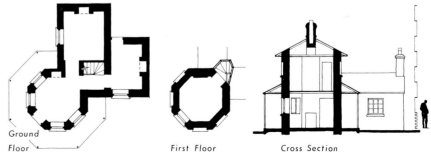

Ground Floor   First Floor   Cross Section

Boughrood Bridge, near **Llys-wen** (Powys) was built in the 1830s. For ten or fifteen years there was no toll house and then this little cottage was added to the side of the bridge. It was designed by the architects T. H. Wyatt and David Brandon. Their unusual plan provides the four rooms which were accepted by the 1840s as normal for a worker's house. Recent internal alterations have made the original position of the staircase uncertain. The occupants in 1851 were John Meredith, aged 28, and his wife Elizabeth, 25. Like William Jones at Llanfair-pwllgwyngyll *(page 21)* the Merediths were cobblers. He was a shoemaker; she was a shoebinder. They had a baby son, aged 8 months.

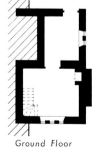

Ground Floor

First Floor

Cross Section

At **Nash Point,** in the parish of **Marcross** (Glamorgan) a lighthouse was built in 1832 on the rocky headland. At first there was only one lightkeeper who lived next to the tower (the nearer house was added after 1851). It was common for heavy responsibilities to be laid on one lowly paid working man. In 1841 he was Rees Palmer, a 45-year old widower with four teenage children. By 1851 three keepers shared the duties. The principal, 30-year old Daniel Daniels, lived here with his wife Mary and two baby sons. They were able to employ a servant, 18-year old Sarah Robert.

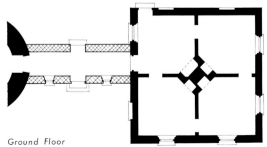

Ground Floor

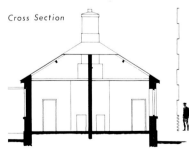

Cross Section

The Pilots Cottages on **Llanddwyn Island** (Anglesey) were built at the end of the 19th century. Their design still follows the traditional *croglofft* form. The pilots were stationed at the south end of the Menai Straits. They took sailing ships up the difficult passage, between shifting sandbanks, to Caernarfon and Y Felinheli (Port Dinorwic). The houses had a relatively short useful life. When they were built the carriage of slates by sea for use all over Britain was already declining in favour of railway transport. The houses are sited on a tidal island, making them inconvenient for other occupants. Today they have become a small museum. One is empty and open to visitors (but note that the *croglofft* ladder has been replaced, for safety, by a narrow stair). Another has been put on display furnished (by the Women's Institutes of Anglesey) at quite a comfortable level with objects suggesting the life of a mariner's household. Not to be missed are the view up into the *croglofft* bedroom, with its original ladder access, and the big communal privy built over a large cess-pit cut into the rock behind the row of houses.

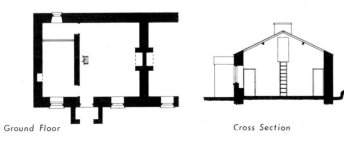

Ground Floor

Cross Section

The road improvements made by the turnpike trusts were felt gradually throughout Wales. Canal building, mainly in South Wales, had much more rapid effects. Between 1790 and 1799 five major canals were built through the valleys of Gwent and Glamorgan to bring down iron from the furnaces at Ystradgynlais and Merthyr Tydfil; tramroads connected the canals to the Hirwaun, Sirhowy and Blaenafon furnaces. The purpose of these systems was strictly industrial but much of their route lay through unspoiled richly wooded countryside. Archdeacon Cox admired the Blaenafon tramroad in 1799: "the (tram) road, sometimes conveyed in a straight line, sometimes winding round the sides of precipices, is a picturesque object" he wrote. On the canals the descent from the heads of the valleys required many locks. The route was dotted with the houses of lock-keepers and maintenance workers. On busy canals, working day and night, at least two keepers were needed for each flight of locks. Where they could do so, such workers lived countrymen's lives, tilling their gardens when traffic was slack, and raising geese and ducks.

Canal companies generally saw their houses as a permanent capital asset, a part of the fixed equipment of their business. So they built to last, often achieving standards which were better than was usual in the area through which the canal passed. This offered a useful model to other local builders.

The Junction House *(left)* at **Pont-y-moel** (Gwent) was built fairly late in the canal era, after 1812. In that year the Brecknock and Abergavenny Company finished the aqueduct across the Afon Llwyd which linked its route to the Monmouthshire Canal. The B & A Company decided to make an architectural feature of the junction between the two canals and provided a home for the official who recorded the passage of barges and assessed the tolls due. Junction House is now preserved by the Torfaen Museum Trust and is open to the public on occasion. The former **Canal Cottage** *(right)* at **Cilfynydd** (Glamorgan) was a typical example of the houses built by the busy Glamorganshire Canal Company, along the lower stretch of its route between Cardiff and Abercynon. Several of these houses survive but scarcely one displays its appearance as built shortly after 1794.

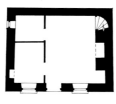

Ground Floor

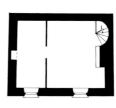
First Floor

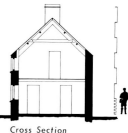
Cross Section

Wern-gerhynt in the parish of **Llanbryn-mair** (Powys) was a weaving settlement which developed in the late eighteenth century. It is in ruins today. Only 4 or 5 houses remain of the 40 or so which existed in 1841. Among the ruins are the walls of two houses, reconstructed in this drawing by Simon Unwin, which belonged to **John Davies I** and his son **John II**.

In the eighteenth century spinning and weaving were the main cottage industries of almost all Wales. Particularly in North Powys and adjacent areas of Clwyd and Gwynedd, woollen cloth was made in quantities large enough to support an export trade to England. Nearly all the processes were carried out by hand in the homes of small-holders and farm workers. The only use of power was fulling, at a local *pandy* or fulling mill, which cleansed and compacted the woven cloth. The road improvements of the turnpike system encouraged this industry for a few years and Llanbryn-mair became an important centre of rural cloth making. But by 1810 enterprising master weavers were gathering country craftsmen into the towns of Powys to work more systematically, though still almost entirely by hand, in specially built factories. At the time of the 1841 census, only a few of the country spinners and weavers were still at work in their cottages.

It is difficult to identify country weavers houses with certainty. In the towns, the factory rooms are easily recognised by their rows of wide windows. There are quite a few houses in country places which have a big window to one room, but only rarely can we say for sure that a spinner or hand-loom weaver earned his or her daily living there. In the case of the Davies's houses there is no doubt. John Davies I was a tailor, aged over 80 in 1841. His son John II and his grandsons John III and Edward were all recorded as weavers by the census. They were among

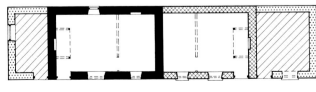

Ground Floor

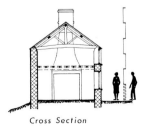

Cross Section

20 weavers still at work in the 40 houses of the hamlet of Werngerhynt. The houses were built on the verges of a part of the old Welshpool to Machynlleth road which had been by-passed by the construction of an early turnpike diversion, some time around 1780-85. John Davies I was probably one of the early settlers. His house was solidly built in stone, most likely as shown here with a roof of rough stone slates, about 1785. His tailor's workshop was at the western *(nearer)* end. About 1815 another house was added, probably for his son John II to set up home with his wife Jane. Their sons John III, aged about 25 in 1841, and Edward, about 15, were provided with another workshop, at the eastern end of the block, when they were old enough to work at their own looms. There were also two grand-daughters, Margaret and Mary, in this three-generation family.

Simon Unwin's drawing uses evidence from other houses in the district to reconstruct features now missing from the John Davies Houses. The enlarged windows of each main room are modelled on another weaver's house at Abercegyr. The roof and fireplace details are based on houses surviving at Werngerhynt. Roofs were framed in rough timbers to carry slates; a roof of this kind was put on to a nearby house in 1786. The fireplaces and chimney hoods were framed up in squared timber and plastered underneath the hood; the smoke was led through a vent high up the gable wall into a stone chimney standing on the apex of the gable.

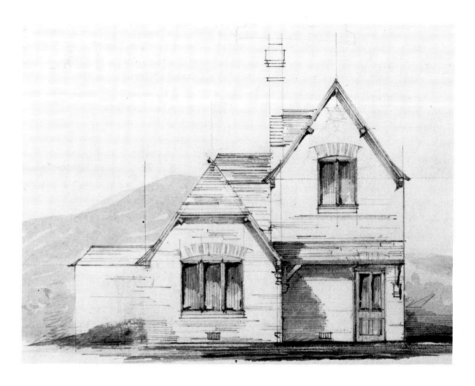

Foryd Station House, near **Rhyl** (Clwyd) was designed in 1858 for a proposed branch off the Vale of Clwyd Railway, then under construction. It was drawn up by R. Lloyd Williams, an architect from Denbigh, to provide one living room and two bedrooms, with booking office, waiting room and men's toilet *(shaded on plan)*. The railways ended the isolation of rural Wales. They spread across the countryside in the years 1855 to 1880, bringing the industrial materials which were to end the local traditions of building, as well as linking Wales to all the markets and influences of England. There is nothing particularly Welsh about this little house. A different design, probably by the same architect, was used for the station built in 1862.

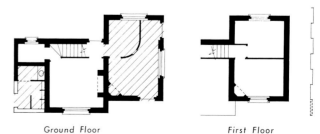

Ground Floor   First Floor

Nant-gwyn Smith Shop near **Pant-y-dŵr** (Powys) was the workplace and home of blacksmith David Thomas for nearly 60 years. In the 19th century the smith's skills were essential to the life of every country community. Smiths shod horses and treated their ailments. They repaired vehicles, made and mended all kinds of farm machinery and tools, household fittings and utensils. They would even iron-tip boots and shoes. The smith shop at Nant-gwyn, now roofless, was built in a damp hollow beside the parish road from St. Harmons to Llanidloes. The little house next to it was

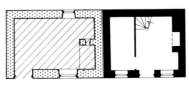

Ground Floor

First Floor

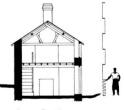

Cross Section

constructed after 1851. For such an important member of the community it was indeed a humble home. David Thomas was about 23 in 1855, when he may have set up his home here with his 19 year old wife Elizabeth. The house has a small kitchen and bedroom on the lower floor and one loft room above. The floor area is about half what we would think they need today. David and Elizabeth had two daughters, Jane Eliza, born 1856, who died in 1880, aged 23, and Sarah Anne, born 1857, who died in 1874, aged 17. Elizabeth also died in 1874, seven months after her daughter, at the age of 39. Such a pattern of early deaths is characteristic of a family susceptible to tuberculosis, a disease aggravated by poor housing. David Thomas lived on to 1911, when he was 79. He and his womenfolk lie buried in the old chapel graveyard which is next to their now-derelict cottage.

The Church School House, Llanycil (Gwynedd) was completed in 1838. It provided both a schoolroom *(shaded on plan)* and a teacher's house. In rural Wales, many places had only informal Sunday schools, mostly run by the chapels with untrained teachers. A child might learn to read there, in Welsh, and much less often to write, but would have no other general education. So the 1210 people in rural Llanycil seemed lucky to acquire this "neat and well-built school-room, lofty and capable of accommodating 50 to 60 children". Unhappily the school was not a success. In 1847 the Inquiry into the State of Education in Wales was told that though "for a short time it was conducted by a master supported by Madam Bevan's Charity, it has been closed for more than five years". In the 1841 census of Llanycil there is no mention of a schoolmaster. The school building was designed in a Tudor style. The master's quarters are extensive, taking up more than two-thirds of the whole school house.

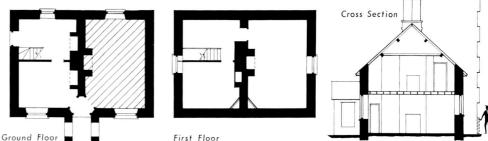

Ground Floor   First Floor   Cross Section

31

The Chapel House, Moriah, Gwyddelwern (Clwyd) illustrates a house type more common in Wales than in England. This neat little cottage, still occupied by the chapel caretaker and his family, was built in 1896. It continues a tradition already seen in rural areas in the 1830's. Some times the chapel house is joined to the chapel itself, usually at the side or the back; sometimes it is set at right angles to the main facade, making a small forecourt. This house sits obediently beside the chapel, literally in its shadow. It is carefully proportioned and solidly built in red Ruabon brick, but possesses only the usual 4 rooms, two up and two down, of the better type of workers' cottage.

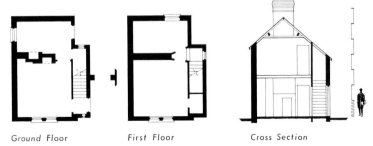

Ground Floor   First Floor   Cross Section

The Limekiln Houses at Belan Locks near
Welshpool (Powys) were built soon after 1800 for
workers at the limekilns on the nearby Canal. Lime
was a valuable product for the improvement of
farmland. The Limekiln Houses are large and solidly
built on three sides in brick. Their northern
elevations, which contain the main windows, are
framed in timber, a practice common in the district.
One pair of houses is plastered, the other boarded,
but on both the decoration of circles is simply
painted; it gives a Picturesque touch much in vogue
in early 19th century cottage building.

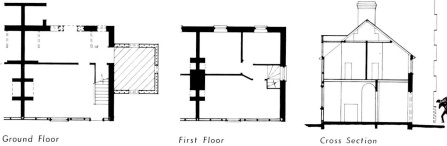

Ground Floor   First Floor   Cross Section

No group of country workers' houses is more varied and ornamental than the lodges built for park gatekeepers. But many of these houses offer quite ordinary accommodation. An 18th century landowner liked his country 'seat' to be surrounded by a landscaped park where deer or cattle could be seen grazing. The park would be enclosed by a high fence or wall. If the owner's wealth allowed there would a servant living at the gates, always ready to open them. Such simple duties required no skill. So often the gate lodge was allocated to a married worker who had another job on the estate. It would be his wife and their growing children who usually opened the gates, dropping a curtsey or knuckling their foreheads to their master as he passed by.

Nantybela Lodge, to **Gwrych Castle, Abergele** (Clwyd) was built about 1821, probably to a design by the architect C. A. Busby. Like the main house the lodge followed the fashion for 'castellated', that is 'castle-like', building originated by Richard Payne Knight, who built Downton Castle, near Ludlow (Shropshire), in 1774-8. Many castellated houses were built in Wales during the following fifty years. Nantybela Lodge has attractive 'Gothick' windows but it is quite a simple house. It had two main rooms, linked by a circular stair.

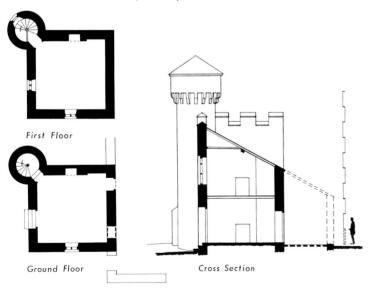

First Floor

Ground Floor

Cross Section

The Lodges to **Dolforgan Hall, Kerry** (Powys) stand on the main road through Kerry village. They were built about 1820-30 in a curious version of the 'Gothick' style. Each window and door opening was extended upwards with a panel of false painted tracery. So the lodges seem to have only one storey. In fact they are similar in form to Llanycil Schoolhouse *(page 31)*. They had two good rooms on the ground floor and three rooms on the floor above, partly within the roof space. The photograph was taken about 100 years ago; both lodges still exist today but in somewhat altered condition.

Ground Floor

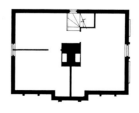

First Floor

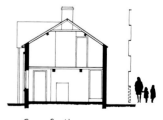

Cross Section

The South Lodge in the parish of **Llandygwydd** (Dyfed) guards the entrance to **Blaenpant House.** It was built before 1815 (the North Lodge opposite was built after that date). It was designed by someone, probably a local builder, who had only a hazy understanding of the styles of architecture then fashionable. Basically the lodge is identical to other traditional cottages in the Teifi valley *(see page 11)* but it has been dressed up externally in a variety of styles. The gable end is treated almost as a temple pediment, showing a touch of Grecian influence. The window lintels are ornamented with drip mouldings, a feature of Tudor and Elizabethan origin, and the central doorway has a semi-circular fanlight, like many of the Georgian town-houses being built at that time. All this 'architecture' was on the surface. Inside the house the arrangement of rooms would have been quite familiar to the lodge keeper and his family.

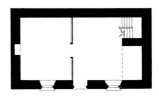

Ground Floor

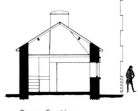

Cross Section

The Golden Lodge to **Kinmel Park**, near **Abergele** (Clwyd) was built in 1868 for William Hughes. The date and his initials appear in several places on the exterior. The lodge was designed by W. Eden Nesfield, one of the major architects of the Victorian period, who also designed the main house at Kinmel which, unhappily, was destroyed by fire in 1975. The lodge is extravagantly ornamented outside, more so than any other house in this booklet, but it was not particularly well planned inside. The position of the staircase is awkward and the elaborate dormer window on this front facade serves no useful purpose.

The gatelodge was a symbol of taste as well as of wealth. Buildings with such a simple purpose could take almost any form, reflecting both the fashions of the day and their owners' preferences. In the 19th century lodges became more and more a status symbol. They lost most of their protective function, being built at the entrances to houses surrounded only by gardens, where there were no park animals to be enclosed.

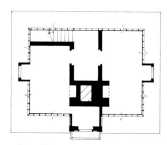

First Floor

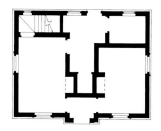

Ground Floor

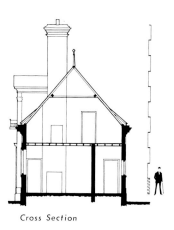

Cross Section

Section Three   House types of the nineteenth century

After 1800 the old traditional ways of building country workers' houses began to give way to new house types and new methods of building. Most of these changes were the result of the industrial revolution. Large numbers of country people were moving to industrial towns and settlements, drawn there by the hope, not always fulfilled, of higher earnings and less hardship. Their migration produced a huge demand for workers' housing in the towns. In its turn that led to a more organised building industry and new ways of building. Machinery was developed to take over at least some of the processes of preparing materials. Components like staircases and windows were simplified and standardised, and house designs were devised which were suitable for building in large numbers. Terraces, in the form of 'row' housing, became as usual for workers' dwellings, as they were for the homes of well-to-do people in places like Bath and the West End of London. In towns many workers' rows were built 'back-to-back'. In country places such a compact space-saving layout was largely unnecessary and it is therefore rare.

Tŷ-Mynydd, Gelli-gaer (Glamorgan) was an isolated dwelling built as an 'encroachment' on the edge of Gelli-gaer Common about 1840. Although it was a single house it was built to exactly the same design as the long rows of iron-workers' and colliers' houses which had been built in towns like Rhymney and Ebbw Vale during the 1830s and 40s. Its symmetrical front, having a central doorway with two windows on either side, also shows the orderliness of industrial influence. Tŷ-Mynydd was demolished about 1972.

Ground Floor

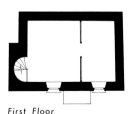

First Floor

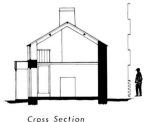

Cross Section

Brick Row, Hawarden (Clwyd) stands on the south side of the main street. It was built before 1815 for workers on the Glynne family's estate. These are excellent houses solidly built with four good rooms, three of which have fireplaces. Over each pair of doors there is a blank opening and an elliptical arch which are purely ornamental. The careful design and use of brick for the front wall is notable; brick was an industrial material, but until 1850 it was taxed. That discouraged its use in places where building stone was available; in fact the rear wall of Brick Row is built in stone. The big windows are made of cast iron, another 'new' material. Downstairs they were fixed so all ventilation was by the door; upstairs one half of the window slides sideways across the other half. The shutters are also original features.

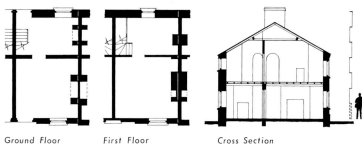

Ground Floor   First Floor   Cross Section

39

Rhiwlas Terrace, Llanfyllin (Powys) is a rare survival. It was built before 1830 in the timber framed construction widely used in North-east Powys. To us this row has the charm of a little country town but it is closely related to the slums of industrial Britain. In some of the largest cities of the early 19th century, poor workers houses were built like this of timber and plaster, with just one room on each floor (the rooms at the back of this row were added later in the 19th century). The upper rooms were reached by ladders placed beside the big open fireplace. As a building Rhiwlas Terrace is every bit as bad as some of the city rows condemned as slums a hundred years ago. This makes it all the more precious as historical evidence.

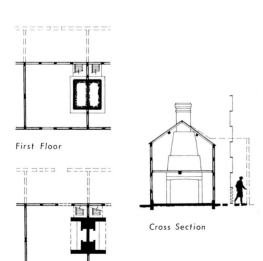

First Floor

Cross Section

Ground Floor

The Terrace, Llanfair Dyffryn Clwyd (Clwyd) offers much the same space as Rhiwlas Terrace *(opposite)* but it was carefully built in good stone before 1830, with attractive Gothick windows, to suit its position facing the village church. The fourth house was projected forward slightly and given a gable to emphasise the centre of the row, but no other variation was made to the repetition of the standard plan. The Terrace is well protected today by its owners, a charitable trust; it has recently been modernised and is a 'listed' historic building. Its survival, like that of Rhiwlas Terrace, long after the demolition of similar dwellings in slum districts of big towns, has a message for us. Slums were not created by poor building design alone. Excessive density of occupation, bad sanitation and uncaring management were more important factors then, and are still so today.

Ground Floor

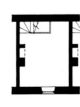

First Floor

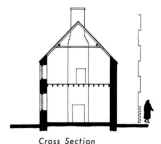

Cross Section

Many travellers in West Wales referred to the use of earth in building the walls of houses, some of which we can still see today. This *clom* construction, the Welsh equivalent of English 'cob', was a skilled craft. Clay, often with some added small gravel, was mixed with short straw, watered and well trodden together. This material was laid in layers on a stone foundation. Each layer was allowed to dry for some days before the next was added, so it took quite a while to build a *clom* house. Properly used and when protected by a thick coating of limewash (renewed every year), *clom* is warm in winter, cool in summer, weather-proof and durable. It is a much better material than the combination of rough branches and mud plaster once used for building squatters' cabins, which followed the pattern of the *tai unnos*.

At **Blaengeuffordd, Capel Bangor** (Dyfed) this substantial dwelling, now demolished, was part of a short row of *clom* houses, once extending to the left of the picture. The house to the right was built later over the *clom* gable wall, which still survives. Though built in a row, this house had many old features, including a huge fireplace with a wickerwork and mud-plaster hood, a narrow stair beside it, and roof trusses made of irregular lengths of rough unsawn timber. It was probably built about 1830 or 1840.

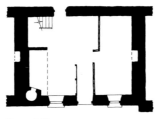

Ground Floor

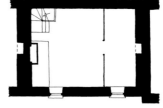

First Floor

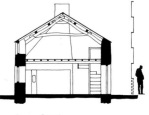

Cross Section

The old house at **Rhyd-trwodd, Tudweiliog** (Gwynedd) was built, perhaps around 1800, in a mixture of stonework (for the gables) and *clom* (for the side walls). It had two rooms and a sleeping loft. In the later 19th century, the roof and side walls were raised slightly and the roof was covered with slates instead of thatch.

Tirpentwys Cottage, in the parish of **Trevethin** (Gwent), stood on high ground between Crumlin and Pontypool where stone was the traditional wall material. Most unusually it had a datestone (1837). Its plan and its near-symmetrical front were just what one might have found in housing rows near the ironworks that surrounded Pontypool. But except for the floorboards, all the timber was rough.

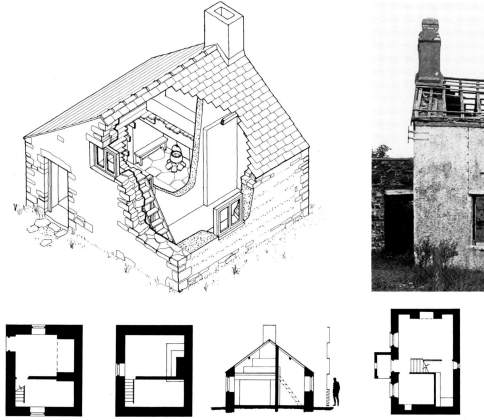

Ground Floor	First Floor	Cross Section

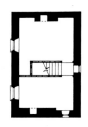
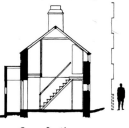

Ground Floor	First Floor	Cross Section

43

Until the early nineteenth century, country land owners and tenant farmers throughout Britain were generally agreed that it was unwise to build houses for any but their most trusted, regular and essential living-out workers. Other farm employees were hired casually, by the week or even the day. When farming prospered there might be work and wages for all. In less happy times casual workers were under-employed for long periods, driving them to apply for aid to the authorities of the parish in which they lived. The land owners and farmers had to finance this aid, by paying a 'poor rate'. They therefore tried to make sure that casual workers did not live in any parish where they paid rates. There were some estate owners who genuinely wanted to improve the living conditions of poor farm workers which writers on rural affairs had condemned. John Wood wrote in 1781 that "habitations of that useful and necessary rank of men, the labourers, were become for the most part offensive both to decency and humanity". But most of those who built on their estates owned so much land in a parish that they could prevent casual workers moving in to it.

In 1834 the poor relief system was re-organised to spread the costs over a whole district. As a result, estate owners became more ready to consider building workers houses on their lands. There was a growing interest in 'model' designs published in the journals of agricultural societies. Many owners used house-building as an aid to firm management. Hard-working, obedient employees were rewarded by a good house. Few owners used housing as a business, in the manner of city landlords, to make profits out of the rents paid by their tenants. Often the designs chosen had a markedly individual character, which we can recognise today wherever it is found on a large estate. Sometimes the houses are plain and solid, sometimes highly ornamented. Almost always they are well built as a long-term investment and a reflection of the owner's worth and wealth. They contribute greatly to the character of our countryside but few of them are protected as 'listed' buildings. They are much threatened by insensitive alterations made in the name of 'improvement'.

Park Houses, Park Street, Ruabon (Clwyd) stand outside the gates to Wynnstay Park, seat of the Wynn family. These houses were built six to a block, but have now been altered. There were two 'back-to-back' houses at either end and two 'through' houses in the middle. The fronts were ornamented in Tudor style, but the soft stone mouldings have decayed and ugly modern metal windows have been put into the openings. **April Cottage, Llanfihangel Aberbythych** (Dyfed) was built after 1839 near the gates to Golden Grove, one of the estates of the Earl of Cawdor. Once there were three houses in this building. Now it is one house. A building of this same unusual form was constructed about 1870 on another Cawdor estate, 50 miles away *(page 48)*.

27-30 Forge Lane, Dyffryn, Newport (Gwent) is a group of houses built in 1828, before the Poor Law reform. They belonged to the powerful Morgan family who controlled all the land and tenancies around their seat at Tredegar Park. There were once six houses (now four) arranged in a U-plan around an open back yard. This road front has a little loggia formed by columns and arches in cast iron. The Morgan family had large interests in the ironworks of western Gwent. The windows once had pretty Gothick glazing bars but these have mostly been 'improved' away now.

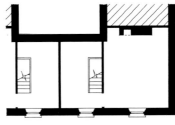

First Floor

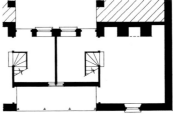

Ground Floor

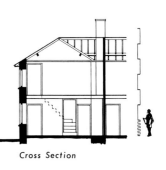

Cross Section

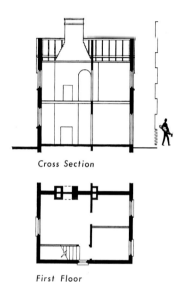

Cross Section

First Floor

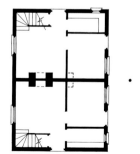

Ground Floor

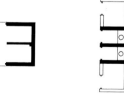

Upper Cottages, Garthmyl, near **Berriew** (Powys) were built on the Garthmyl Hall estate in 1860. Unusually the ridge of the roof runs above the wall separating the two houses. There is a practical reason for this feature. All the rain water from the roof drains to the back corners and thence to a well behind the houses. This arrangement accentuates the box-like shape of the simple, solid building. Plainly these houses and others like them in Garthyml village were an investment, expected to last, as indeed they have for 120 years, without major repair. Even the windows survive unaltered. At the back, on the line between the two gardens, there is a pump (now disused) from the well, then a small wash-house once fitted with a copper, and two earth-closets flanked by ash-pits. Such practical attentions to sanitation suggest that these were 'model' cottages, based on a design by a sanitary pioneer.

Venton Cottages, Castlemartin (Dyfed) end our survey. The lives of many country workers ended during their working years, as a result of accident or illness. Those who became infirm generally had to seek help from relatives, or go into the workhouse. There men and women, even elderly married couples, were strictly separated. Lord Cawdor's estate offered a much more humane alternative — the estate almshouse. There were four separate dwellings here; those at the ends had two rooms while the two in the middle, sharing the central porch, provided bed-sitting rooms with a little kitchen space at the back. The material was solid concrete, just being tried out in the 1870s as a modern substitute for *clom*. Lord Sudeley also used concrete on his estate at Tregynon (Powys). As things turned out concrete proved durable but very cold and liable to trouble with condensation. It was not a good choice for old people's houses.

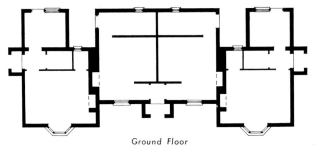

Ground Floor